THE VILLA OF THE MYSTERIES IN POMPEII

General characteristics

IN the last three decades of the 2nd cent. B.C. it became the fashion, among the Roman aristocracy, to own a summer residence in Campania. All along the coastline stretching from the Phlegraean Fields as far as Punta della Campanella, the furthest end of the Sorrento peninsula, major figures in Roman history built themselves villas, i.e. country estates comprising main house, grounds and outhouses. Among these are Scipio the African, who owned a villa in *Liternum*, his daughter Cornelia, who raised and educated her children at Miseno, the famous Gracchi brothers, Marius, Sulla, Pompeius, Caesar, Brutus and Cicero. Luxurious villas to which wealthier Roman citizens used to retire for respite from the hustle and bustle of city life sprang up like mushrooms, at first right on top of hills and then closer and closer to the beach thanks to the development of a new kind of mortar that could even be used for constructions underwater. These houses had gardens with impressive fountains and waterworks, olympic-size swimming-pools, magnificently decorated baths, ornamental statues, wall paintings and mosaic floors. From the surviving ruins, however abundant, the visitor can barely get an idea of the architectural variety of these buildings and the wealth of their decorations. The lavish recreations of the Villa dei Papiri and the Roman villa uncovered near Naples at Oplontis (Torre Annunziata) which Paul Getty built himself in Malibu (California) are probably the nearest thing to the actual dimensions of those mansions and the magnificence of their decorations.

Scene of sacrifice (alcove B in cubiculum no. 4).

From Pompeii, House of the Centenary. (National Museum, Naples)

IN addition to the smart summer residences used by the Romans for holidaying (*otium*) there was also another category of villa, the *villa rustica*, which was a farmhouse used for agricultural purposes. Given the exceptional fertility of the soil in Campania and the mild climate affording several harvests a year, the area also became dotted with countless estates of this kind. The ruins of hundreds of ancient farmhouses have been uncovered in the area all round Pompeii (Boscoreale, Boscotrecase, Scafati, Angri, Terzigno), although most of them were simply stripped of their precious objects and paintings and then promptly reburied.

A typical *villa rustica*, which was usually a medium-size construction, was divided into a residential section inhabited by the owner (*the pars urbana*) and a second part (*the pars rustica*) reserved for the servants of the household. The latter part generally included a number of stables, various kinds of workshops and the servants' lodgings.

In some cases, the *villa rustica* was the landlord's home, but more often it was run by a tenant-farmer (*vilicus*). The farm-hands were for the most part slaves, but on occasion freemen were employed. Most of the farms in the surroundings of ancient Pompeii were wine-making establishments because the slopes of Mount Vesuvius and the hills both all round and within the town were thickly

Boscoreale, Villa Regina. Wine-cellar with 18 large earthenware jars (capacity 10,000 litres) buried in the ground up to their necks.

overgrown with vines. Ancient authors have handed down to us the names of the main grape species that used to be grown in the area: the large-grape *Aminea*, the *Pompeiana*, the *Holconia* and the *Vennuncula*. Large quantities of oil, fruit and cereals were grown and cattle-raising was also widespread. There are examples of farming estates completed by a sumptuous residential annex, and some lavish seaside summer residences were encircled by extensive fields and equipped with all the workshops and implements needed to process all sorts of agricultural produce. The *Villa dei Misteri*, or Villa of Mysteries, in Pompeii is a typical suburban villa of the kind frequently found in the area lying at the foot of Mount Vesuvius and combines the comforts of a luxury country residence and the production facilities of a farm.

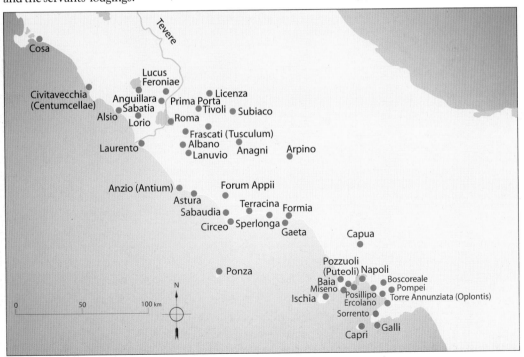

Central Italy: areas dotted with villas.

Plan of the Villa of Mysteries

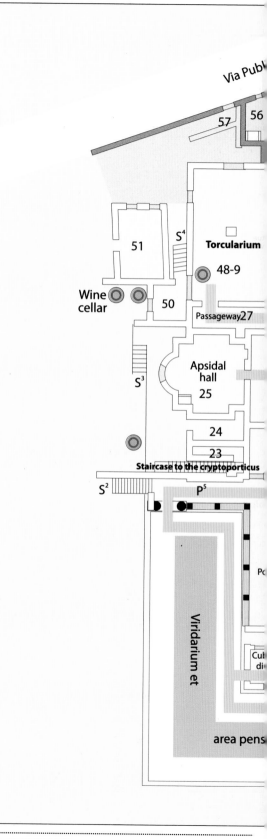

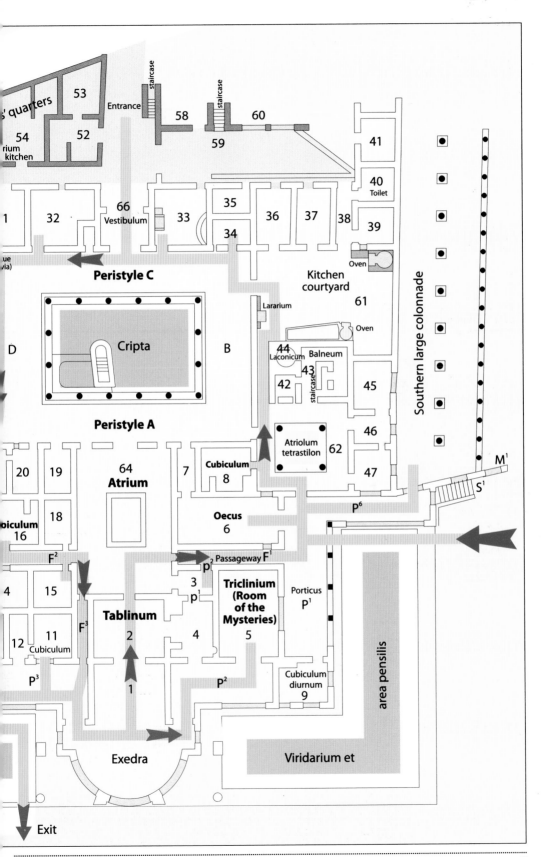

Servants' quarters
53
Entrance
staircase
58
staircase
60
54
atrium kitchen
52
59
41
40 Toilet
1
32
66 Vestibulum
33
35
34
36
37
38
39
statue (via)
Oven
Kitchen courtyard
61
Peristyle C
Lararium
Cripta
B
Oven
D
44 Laconicum
Balneum
43
staircase
42
45
Peristyle A
62
Atriolum tetrastilon
46
47
20
19
64
Atrium
7
Cubiculum 8
M¹
18
Oecus 6
P⁶
S¹
Cubiculum 16
F²
P¹
4
15
F³
Passageway F¹
p²
3
p¹
Triclinium (Room of the Mysteries)
Porticus P¹
12
11 Cubiculum
Tablinum
2
4
5
Cubiculum diurnum 9
P³
1
P²
area pensilis
Exedra
Viridarium et
Exit

1. Discovery and unearthing

HAPHAZARD digging was started by the owner of the site between 1909 and 1910; later on, extensive excavation work was conducted in line with exacting scientific procedures in 1929-30, after the site had been expropriated by the Italian government. In a first report on the villa published by the archaeologist Amedeo Maiuri in 1931, the complex was described and reproduced in magnificent colour pictures.

The discovery at once aroused great interest because of a superb fresco cycle whose interpretation has remained the object of debate to this day and from which the villa draws its name.

As much fewer household and luxury items were unearthed than was to be expected considering the magnificence of the estate, archaeologists have conjectured that the smart residential part of the complex was not in use at the time of the eruption. In fact, extensive reconstruction and refurbishing work appears to have been in progress. Numerous farming implements and materials among the finds suggest that only the *pars rustica* of the estate and the slaves' lodgings were inhabited. This detail is also confirmed by the skeletons of a number of people probably servants that were uncovered in the rustic part of the complex. The rests of a victim of the eruption were found in the vestibule right at the entrance to the villa. These are a young girl who was probably trying to escape across the fields when she was stifled by the gas and buried under the ashes erupting from the volcano at the very last stage of the disaster. The body of a man was found in room no. 35, where he had probably hoped to find shelter from the shower of ashes and lapilli raging outside. A plaster cast of the man's body was obtained during the excavation work: the hollow left in the hardened ash mass by the gradual decomposition of the body was filled with liquid chalk, thus recreating the shape of the dead man's body. Three more women appear to have sought shelter in upstairs rooms, but as the staircase collapsed under the weight of the ashes and lapilli they had no way out and were prevented from escaping. When the floor of the room also gave way under the pressure, they found themselves in the room below (no. 55), where archaeologists have found remains of their bodies.

Four victims were also found in the *cryptoporticus* (covered underground gallery) of the house.

Plaster cast of a victim - An ostiary.

A view of the exterior.

2. Description of the complex

THE Villa of Mysteries is situated a few hundred metres outside the city walls and is in good state of repair.

As it was built on a steeply sloping site, it was necessary to create an artificial terrace supported by the vaults of the underground gallery (*cryptoporticus*). In this way the complex could be built on the sunniest part of the site, which also commanded the finest view of the area.

The original layout of the villa dates back to the first half of the 2nd cent. B.C. Major restructuring work was carried out about 70-60 B.C., during which period most of the walls and floors were decorated.

The farmhouse was added to the residential complex in the 1st century B.C. and suffered heavy damage during the disastrous earthquake that struck Pompeii in 62 B.C. At the time of the eruption of Mt Vesuvius in 79 A.D., the last owner of the estate was completely refurbishing the villa in order to bring it in line with the tastes of the time and his own needs. This work was still under way when Mount Vesuvius erupted.

The overall layout of the Villa of Mysteries complex is similar to that of most of the other villas in the area. Accordingly, it commands a fine view of the open sea as far as the isle of Capri and the mountainous profile of the Sorrento peninsula.

Its main entrance gate gave onto the *Via Superior*, a side-street of *Via dei Sepolcri* that runs across the built-up area of Pompeii passing through the *Porta Ercolano* city gate, and is consequently situated on the front right opposite to that from which visitors are currently admitted to the complex (1). To follow the same path of an ancient visitor, we have to cross the complex and start our visit from the opposite side of the current entrance, which gives access to the villa's rustic farm section.

Two arched passageways form a vestibule (66) on either side of which a doorway leads to the rustic part of the villa. One noteworthy detail is the vestibule floor, which is made from lavic stone that was also used to build the streets of Pompeii, thus allowing cars to enter the household and be unloaded not far from its rustic section.

The street leading to the entrance of the villa.

Traces left by a door.

Visual reconstruction of the original appearance of the Villa of the Mysteries.

Saint-Romain-en-Gal (Rhône). Mosaic.

A winepress.

The rooms numbered from 52 to 60 were built in the Augustan Age as lodgings for the servants. In one of them the excavators found the seal of one L. Istacidius Zosimus, freedman (i.e. a former slave) of the powerful Istacidii family from Pompeii. It is assumed that L. Istacidius Zosimus was either the owner of the villa or, more probably, the overseer (*procurator*) in charge of the reconstruction work in progress there at the time of its destruction.

To the right of the entrance door, the visitor reaches the wine-making premises (48-49). One of the rooms, which was used to store must, contains a *torcular*, i.e. a winepress. Only one of the two presses that were found in room 49 has so far been restored. Grapes were pressed as soon as the calcatores, sturdy men who treaded them with their bare feet, had completed their job. The treaded grapes were filled into baskets and placed under the press. Pressing grapes with this sort of implement was a fairly complex job. A thick wooden pole with a ram head at one end (*prelum*) was pushed down by means of a winch (*sucula*) so that it would

press on the wicker baskets placed under it. From the masonry basin in which it was collected, the resulting must flowed into an underground cistern through a duct running all along the northern wall. The

iron parts of the winepress are exhibited in a display case fixed to one of the walls.

Five iron bill-hooks, two pick-axes, a how, a shovel, a hammer, an oven rake and a few nails are found in room 32, whose walls are painted in 4th style (50-70 B.C.) with inserted decorations in previous styles (2nd and 3rd). The *vilicus* was in charge of all these farming implements and used to distribute them to the farmhands before they set out to work in the fields every day.

The bronze seal of L. Istacidius Zosimus, a freedman of the Istacidii family.

Pompeii House of the Vettii, the triclinium. Cupids at work in a vineyard.

Scene II. Sacrifice and libation. A p[...] [...]on the left).

The kitchen area (33-37) is reached through the door on the left of the entrance.

In the courtyard (61) the visitor can see two ovens, the *lararium* (a small temple usually placed near the kitchen) and a large toilet (40).

A small bathing area (42-44) was laid out close to the kitchen in the 2nd century B.C. in order to tale advantage of the steam produced by the ovens there.

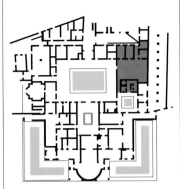

It includes the following rooms: an *apoditerium* (changing room), a *tepidarium* (a room kept at a moderate temperature), which later on was partitioned in order to build a staircase leading upstairs, and a round room (44) named *laconicum* (the sweating room).

The walls of the latter are covered with *tegulae mammatae*, i.e. special terracotta tiles with breast-like projections forming an interspace through which hot air was made to flow thus heating the room.

When necessary, a bronze brazier could be lit to increase the temperature. To avoid saturating the room with steam, air was discharged through four cylindrical exhaust channels in the vault.

A sacrifice. (Alcove B in cubiculum no. 4)

An oven, an open fire and a lararium. (drawing by R. Oliva)

In front of the baths is a small *atrium* (62) where the bathers used to rest. From there, they proceeded to a bedroom (*cubiculum*) (8) with 2nd style wall paintings (2nd 1st cent. B.C.) featuring harmonious illusionistic architectural structures.

The adjoining room is a large reception hall (*oecus*) (6) where the rests of ancient pictorial landscapes can still be seen above a number of rectangular niches.

The latter originally housed wooden panels framed by painted friezes featuring various kinds of arms.

Through a doorway the visitor enters the southern ambulatory of a Colonnade (P) that runs along three sides of the 'urban' part of the villa and was used for taking walks and enjoying a charming view of the surrounding landscape.

When the 2nd style was still in use, this colonnade formed a right angle with its western wing, but in the Augustan Age a daytime cubiculum (9) was built right at the junction of

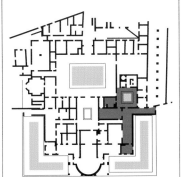

these two wings.

This newly-created room was an ideal place for a rest and has three marble-silled windows giving onto a beautiful terrace. Its undecorated walls suggest that building work was in progress in it at the time of the eruption.

Festoon with leaves. (detail of the wall decoration in oecus no. 6)

Scene III. Silen in the guise of a musician.

Room 1 (the *exedra*) has colonnades all along three sides and a fine hanging garden. Its structures rest on those of the *cryptoporticus* (a covered underground gallery) that was created to even out the surface of the sloping ground.

It is completed by a semicircular veranda with three larger and two smaller windows that command a view of unrivalled beauty of the surrounding countryside and the bay.

Walking across room 1, the visitor reaches the *tablinum* (2), an open living-room which was an integral component of any upper-class Roman residence. This originally housed the family archives (see Plinius, *Naturalis Historiae*, XXXV, 2-7), but later on it was turned into a living and reception room where the master of the house used to receive his guests or people coming to pay him homage or lay particular requests before him (*clientes*). In other residences, this part of the house leads directly into the *atrium*, but here, in the Villa of the Mysteries, the two rooms

have no longer been communicating since the Augustan Age, when the tablinum was walled up and turned into a hall with magnificent 3rd style wall paintings (20 B.C.-50 A.D.) on a black background. The *dado* (lower part of the wall) features a pergola; a *predella* (a stripe between the dado and the intermediate horizontal area of

the wall) is decorated with small Egyptian figures; the intermediate area itself features miniature Dionysiac symbols (such as masks, horn-shaped drinking-cups and *thyrsi*). The floor mosaic is made from white tesserae with parallel rows of white tesserae. Following the earthquake of 62 B.C., a new entrance door was opened to interconnect the *tablinum* to room 4. As the holes in the ceiling are by enough to fit beams, it is assumed that the owner was about to build an upper floor when the 79 A.D. eruption stifled all life in the villa.

The tablinum. Details of 3rd style wall paintings.

Room 4 was the master's bedroom (*cubiculum*) and was reached through an anteroom containing an alcove used as wardrobe and a double alcove in which the beds were placed. The 2nd style paintings in the anteroom create the illusion that the walls are lined with marble slabs while the alcoves are decorated with painted square-shaped panels (*pinakes*) and statues. The door leading into the *tablinum* (2) does not date from the same time as the paintings, but was opened on the occasion of later refurbishing work after which the northern alcove could no longer be used. The door leading into room 3, originally another bedroom, was probably opened on the same occasion, when room 3, which has excellent 2nd style wall paintings, was turned into the anteroom of the master's bedroom. A small door in its southern wall leads into the famous room after which the villa is named.

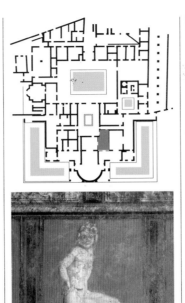

Cubiculum no. 4. A dancing satyr and, on the right, a priestess.

2nd style paintings on the walls of room no. 3.

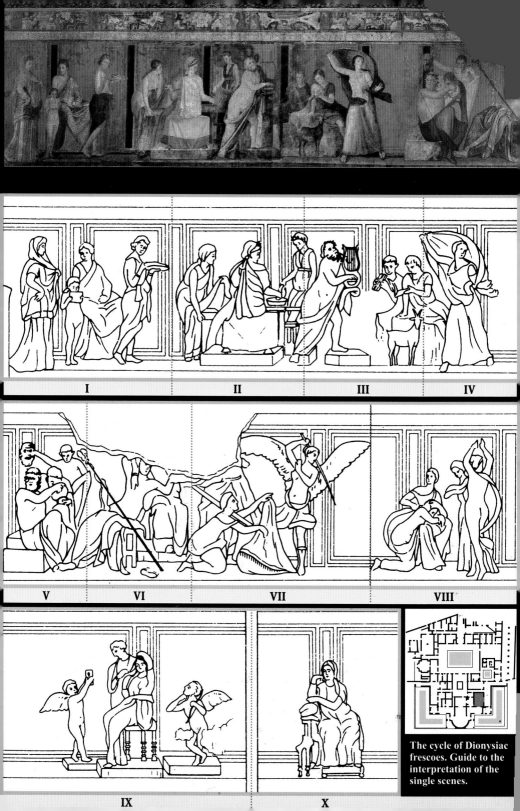

I   II   III   IV

V   VI   VII   VIII

IX   X

The cycle of Dionysiac
frescoes. Guide to the
interpretation of the
single scenes.

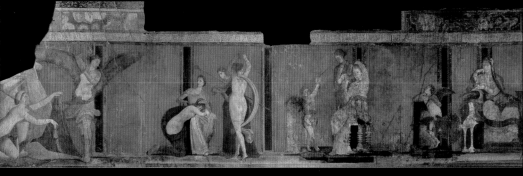

THE DIONYSIAC MYSTERIES

Triclinium 5

Triclinium 5 (also termed the 'Room of Mysteries') is decorated with a magnificent large-scale wall painting which is a copy of a 2nd or 3rd century Greek-Hellenistic original by a Campanian artist active around the mid-1st century B.C. Scholars from all over the world have endeavoured and indeed are still trying to establish the real meaning of these marvellous images. In the opinion of some, the frescoes depict a theatrical scene, because the characters seem to be treading a sort of narrow stage, but in line with the most-widely accepted interpretation they represent a young girl's initiation into the Bacchic 'mysteries'. The Dionysiac (or, in Rome, Bacchic) cult was widespread throughout Campania. As they offered worshippers an escape from reality, Bacchic rites spread rapidly, in part due to the climate of unease caused by radical social change in the 2nd century B.C. As the rites concerned were also attended by women and slaves, it was rumoured that promiscuous sexual encounters were practised during bacchanals and that the followers of Bacchus had joined to form a dangerous secret sect. The Roman Senate passed a law (*senatusconsultum*) which prohibited the celebration of secret rites without the prior consent of the Senate and enforced the death penalty in respect of offenders of this legal provision. Apparently this law was never enforced in Pompeii, where the cult was regularly practised.

The renowned French historian Paul Veyne has recently suggested that the frescoes do not feature Bacchic rites, but rather the wedding of an upper-class girl. The mysterious frescoes can be 'read' starting from the right. The first group shows two women and a reading boy according to many scholars young Dionysus reading aloud

Scene X. The "Domina", the mistress of the house.

the ritual prescriptions in the presence of his mother Semele and his sister Ino. In Veyne's opinion, the boy is the bride's younger brother reading the classics at the instruction of his private tutor while his mother is standing on the left overseeing her son's progress. Another woman is seen on the right, carrying a tray containing sliced food. Traditionally, this woman

has been thought to symbolise Spring offering sacred flat cakes to Demetra, the goddess of vegetation. In Veyne's eyes, however, she is a slave carrying a sesame bannock, a dish that was traditionally offered

Scene VII. The unveiling of the phallus.

to wedding guests for propitiatory purposes. The next group includes three women busying themselves around a number of pots into which one of them is pouring water. Currently they are either held to be personifications of three Seasons (Winter is wrapped up in a mantle, Autumn is the woman pouring water into the pot, and Summer is the one on the left), or as a priestess (the woman turning her back on the viewer) placed between her servants. In Veyne's interpretation the scene features the preparation of the wedding bath; among the Romans, a young lady used to have a ritual bath both before and after her first sexual rapport. The next group includes an old Silen with a laurel crown and a lyre and a shepherd and a shepherdess nourishing a kid. According to some scholars, the Silen symbolises cosmic harmony, whilst the shepherds are Pan and a Panisca, with whom Dionysus used to associate. According to Veyne, the presence of a Silen is linked to the musicians that were generally hired for every wedding ceremony. Next to this group is a majestic female figure holding the hem of a billowing mantle that some scholars identify with Aura, the personification of wind and mother of Dionysus. In Veyne's opinion, the woman is frightened by the mask in the hands of a figure of the group painted on the wall opposite the entrance. This group includes another Silen with an ivy crown and a young satyr who is drinking (or simply looking down into the bottom of the cup?); behind them is another satyr who is holding up a mask probably for fun. This scene has been variously interpreted: on the one hand it could depict a dancing competition in which Silen has won a silver cup; on the other, it might suggest a mysterious revelation that the younger satire has 'descried' on the bottom of the cup. According to Veyne, the Satyr is simply offering his young companion a drink in order to introduce him to the pleasures of wine-drinking.

In the next scene, which is incomplete, Dionysus is resting on Ariadne's lap; he is evidently drunk (to the point of losing a sandal). This scene is the clue to the whole pictorial cycle and is accordingly situated opposite the entrance to the room. Initiation rites are in progress all round the central figure, namely Dionysus himself. According to Veyne, Dionysus is overwhelmed by a strong passion for his  bride and the scene with Dionysus in a central position symbolises married love. The very fact

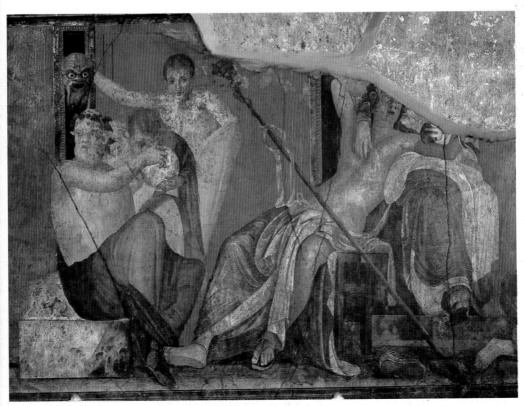

Scene V and VI. Silen giving the satyrs to drink Dionysus and Ariadne.

Scene IX. The wedding toilet.

that Ariadne, upon whose legs he is resting, seems to be enthroned above him like a queen is interpreted as the sign of a happy fertile future life for the bride. In the next group, a crouching woman is seen unveiling a phallus, a symbol of the generating power of nature; the veiled phallus is contained in a sort of wicker basket and was usually presented to the initiate at the beginning of the rites. According to the traditional interpretation of the pictorial cycle, the winged woman with a long cane that appears in the next scene alludes to flagellation, a common rite in the Dionysiac cult. The next scene shows a young girl (the initi-

ate?) seeking shelter in the arms of a woman who appears to be protecting her (probably from the winged woman who is about to lash her). Veyne conversely suggests that the phallus and the scantly dressed, frightened girl in the arms of her wet-nurse are intended to suggest that the bride is frightened by the thought of her wedding night. The following scene features a dancing naked woman with tambourines; she is turning her back on the viewer and behind her is another woman with a thyrsus.

The following scenes shows a beautiful young girl combing her hair. Most scholars have agreed that she is a bride who is

dividing her hair into six locks, as was the custom on the wedding-day. Others are inclined to think that the scene depicts Venus at her dressing-table. The last figure, which appears isolated in a corner between two doors, is a seated woman who is either assumed to be the Domina, the mistress of the house, or, according to the more recent inter-pretation, the bride's mother supervising the arrangements for the imminent wedding ceremony.

Scene VIII. The flagellated and the bacchante.

Cubiculum no. 16, alcove "B". 2nd style wall decoration.

As visitors leave the south-western wing of the colonnade (P3) running along three sides of the residential part of the villa and walk across the exedra (1), they reach the north-western section of the residence. This includes numerous bedrooms that were probably used to accommodate guests at the villa. The first room is a daytime cubiculum (10) matching no. 9 symmetrically. Like that one, it gives onto a hall whose three windows have low marble sills. An additional cubiculum (11) opens out onto the colonnade (P3) through a short passageway (12) used as a vestibule. The north, east and south walls of the latter are decorated with 3rd style paintings on a black background. A similar passageway (13) is the anteroom to cubiculum 14, in which both the ancient floor and the 2nd style decorations of the upper part of the southern wall are preserved. A prominent detail is the elaborate gable of an architectural *aedicula* (shrine for a small statue).

During extensive restructuring work carried out in the Augustan Age, the remaining parts of the walls were covered with 3rd style decorations.

The 2nd style decorations in cubiculum 15 have remained almost intact and unaltered to this day. Their most impressive feature is an illusionistic architectural scene featuring the columned façade of an imaginary building with colonnades drawn in perspective. Originally, this room led onto the atrium (64), but during the rebuilding work necessitated by the 62 B.C. earthquake the door was walled up in part and turned into a window. Work was in under way in passageway F1 when the eruption of Mt Vesuvius occurred in 79 A.D.

The last bedroom in this part of the villa is the cubiculum with two alcoves (16), a particularly sumptuous summer room whose 2nd style wall decoration and original floor are almost entirely preserved. The two doors of this room gave onto the

northern passageway (F2) and the northern colonnade (P4) which is preceded by an ante-

room (17). The central part of the ceiling above the two beds is vaulted. The bedroom was separated from the anteroom by a three-leaf door reproduced in a plaster cast. Its illusionistic architectural decorations, which feature arcades and a door, are among the most noteworthy specimens of perspective

drawing handed down to us from antiquity.

Cubiculum no. 16. 2nd style architectural wall paintings.

The atrium and, in the background, the villa's peristyle.

The peristyle.

A Nile landscape in the atrium.

Lastly, the visitor reaches the large peristyle (65), which was originally accessed directly from the main entrance to the villa. As compared to other upper-class Pompeii residences dating from the same time, in which the peristyle is usually situated immediately past the atrium, this is an innovative layout which according to the Augustan architect Vitruvius was adopted for numerous luxury villas when wealthier Romans developed a distinctive preference for the refined Hellenistic architectural style; direct access into a courtyard lined with colonnades is typical of a particular kind of oriental house.

The villa's peristyle is a rectangular courtyard with sixteen Doric columns linked together by a balustrade (*pluteus*) which is half the height of the columns themselves. From the peristyle the visitor enters room 26, which was the anteroom of the apsidal hall (25).

At the far end of the northern colonnade is room 23, from where a staircase leads down into the majestic underground gallery in which archaeologists found the bodies of four victims who had tried to find refuge from the eruption.

To reach the exit the visitor again walks across the atrium (64), because this, as mentioned before, is situated in an inverse position with respect to the classical villa design. Following the restructuring work carried out after the 62 B.C. earthquake, it became a passageway linking together the different sectors of the building complex. Originally there were thirteen doors, but some of

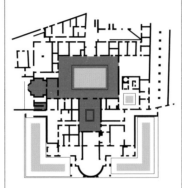

them were subsequently walled up (while the wooden door wings were left in place as fake doors) and some were simply narrowed. The atrium is in the Tuscan style, which means that it has no columns and that the roof is pitched inward. A large basin (*impluvium*) is situated in the middle of the room to collect the rainwater running through an opening in the roof (*compluvium*).

The water thus collected was used for various household purposes. Its wall paintings have severely deteriorated, but a few traces of the pictorial decoration are still preserved in rectangular areas that originally contained painted panels (*pinakes*) framed by ornamented bands showing various kinds of arms. The caricaturistic graffiti of one Rufus, portrayed with a wreath on his head, is visible behind a glass panel on the northern wall along with the inscription "*Rufus est*".

The atrium decoration.

Graffiti caricatures.

Scene VIII. The bacchante.